JUNK-BOX JEWELRY

25 DIY LOW COST (OR NO COST) JEWELRY PROJECTS

First published in North America 2012 by Zest Books
35 Stillman Street, Suite 121, San Francisco, CA 94107
www.zestbooks.net
Created and produced by Zest Books, San Francisco, CA

Typeset in Avenir and Gotham
Teen Nonfiction / Crafts & Hobbies / Clothing & Dress

Library of Congress Control Number: 2011942759

ISBN: 978-0-9827322-6-7

CREDITS
EDITORIAL DIRECTOR/BOOK EDITOR: Hallie Warshaw
CREATIVE DIRECTOR: Hallie Warshaw
ART DIRECTOR/COVER DESIGN: Hallie Warshaw
GRAPHIC DESIGN: Marissa Feind
RESEARCH EDITOR: Nikki Roddy
MANAGING EDITOR/PRODUCTION EDITOR: Pam McElroy
ADDITIONAL TEXT WRITTEN BY: Onnesha Roychoudhuri and Ann Edwards

Manufactured in China
LEO 10 9 8 7 6 5 4 3 2 1
4500351203

Bloomsbury Publishing Plc.
50 Bedford Square
London
WC1B 3DP
www.bloomsbury.com

JUNK-BOX JEWELRY

25 DIY LOW COST (OR NO COST) JEWELRY PROJECTS

Sarah Drew

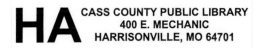

INTRODUCTION

Fashion is always changing (which is why you'd better hurry up and get that pair of ankle boots now!), so it's kind of unbelievable that from the dawn of civilization until today, jewelry has really never gone out of style.

From prehistoric America to ancient Egypt to medieval Milan, people and shiny objects have gone together like peanut butter and jelly, like kings and crowns, like earlobes and earrings. In fact, a recent discovery in North Africa seems likely to prove that even as far back as 80,000 years ago[1] (that is over 30,000 years before *homo sapiens* even arrived on the scene!) our ancestors were fashioning decorative beads out of seashells.

A lot has happened in the intervening ten millennia, but decorative beads are still a solid option for a Friday night party. You can't purchase blocks of real estate with beads anymore, but in most other respects we use beads in exactly the same way that we always have. And what goes for beads also holds true for necklaces, rings, bracelets, tiaras, brooches, pendants … everything! We wear jewelry to symbolize love, or social class, or a high school class, or a sports championship—but we also, even more basically, wear jewelry because it makes us look good and makes our outfits better. Humans just love shiny objects.

Since jewelry has been such a universal element of human life, it's a pretty safe bet that if it *can* be done it probably has been (neck-lengthening necklaces? Check! Earlobe-stretching plugs? Check!)—but that doesn't mean that there's no room for originality here. In fact, that's one of the key reasons why making your own jewelry is so exciting: Every piece you make has never been made before. Even though you're taking part in a tradition that is older even than mankind itself, every piece that you make is totally, 100 percent unique.

---

[1] http://www.sciencecodex.com/prehistoric_jewelry_dates_back_82_000_years

In this book we've compiled ideas that use an incredible variety of everyday items—including old magazine pages, sea glass, vintage lace, and beach stones—and, borrowing from this amazing shared history of human creativity and invention, come up with some really exciting ways to recombine and reinvent these elements for almost any occasion. So whether you want to complement an amazing piece of fabric, highlight a beautiful stone, or just experiment with your toolbox on a lazy Sunday afternoon, it's our hope that you'll always be able to find creative inspiration here.

TABLE OF CONTENTS

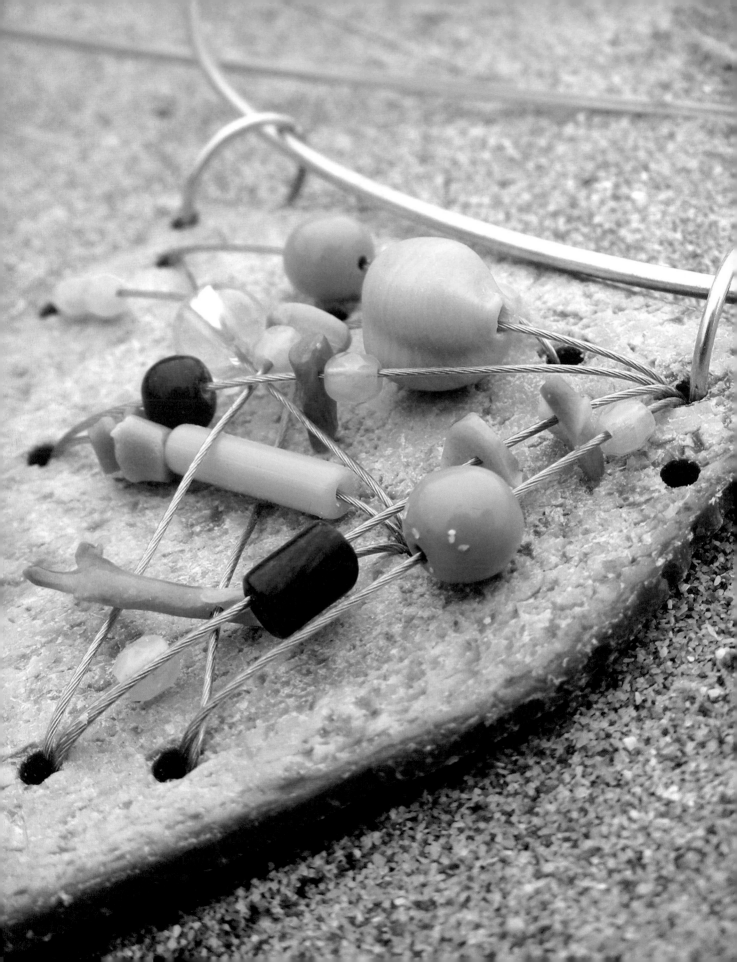

GETTING STARTED

WHAT YOU'LL NEED

The good news? You probably already have most of the stuff you need to make awesome jewelry. The bad news? Okay, there's actually no bad news. You may just have to buy some supplies on the cheap from your local craft store or online (see the "Useful Websites" section on page 100 at the back of the book).

TOOLS

Pliers
This'll be your most-used tool and you can get a great pair for under $10 (look for the kind that have a wire cutter). Use them to shape, bend, and cut wire. We recommend buying two pairs of pliers (try one pair of round-nosed and one pair of flat-nosed pliers) because it makes tasks like bending open jump rings (see page 14) a *lot* easier. Also, use the round-nosed pliers when making loops and curves and the flat-nosed pair to grip/hold the wire and when using crimps (see page 14).

Scissors
Always good to have around, these come in handy for projects that use fabric and lace. One larger pair of shears and a smaller pair of nail or manicure scissors are all you need for the projects in this book.

Dremel Tool or Hand Drill
There are a few projects in this book that call for drilling holes in plastic pieces so that you can string them on necklaces and bracelets. If you're a crafty person always making something, you may be ready to invest in a Dremel tool— it does everything you can imagine, from drilling to sanding and polishing. You can usually find one for around $50. (You could probably convince Mom or Dad that it's a great thing to have around the house.) If you do use a drill for these projects,

remember to *always* wear safety goggles and *always* get an adult to help. No drill? No problem. There's this magical stuff called Shrinky Dinks (see "Useful Websites" on page 100 for ordering info). It's basically plastic that you can cut and design any way you like, then pop in the oven and shrink to beautiful, jewelry-sized proportions. Just remember to put your holes in the plastic (use a standard paper hole punch) before you bake it. Ta-da. All ready to go and you didn't have to drill a thing.

File
There are lots of projects in this book that use jewelry wire. It's a great material, but the ends can be a little sharp. It's a good idea with any of the wire projects to file down sharp edges so that they don't scratch your skin. Use a nail file or a piece of fine sandpaper.

Crochet Hook
Different sizes will give you different looks. For a looser woven design, get a bigger hook. For a tighter weave, go smaller. These are available at any craft or sewing store, and you can get a set of different sized plastic hooks pretty inexpensively.

Glue
Helps you keep it together. For the projects in this book, you'll need regular white glue, super glue, and some clear-drying craft glue.

OTHER DOODADS

Lobster Clasps
No, they don't taste good when dipped in butter, but these little clasps are the perfect way to keep your necklaces and bracelets securely attached to your neck and wrists. Shaped a little like lobster claws, you can find these in almost any craft store, and they're easy to attach to your projects using jump rings (see page 14).

Jump Rings

They look totally boring, but they're the secret weapon in any jewelry-making genius' arsenal. You can use these small metal rings to connect chains to beads, clasps to chains … anything to anything, really. Using two sets of pliers, bend open the rings, slide on whatever you need to attach, then bend them closed again. Voilà!

Jewelry Wire

If you want to be super fancy, you can find sterling silver and real gold jewelry wire, but it's a lot cheaper to get the silver- or gold-coated brass or copper wire and it works just as well. Each individual project will specify the gauge, or thickness, of the wire you'll need. No matter what the project says, the key is to find the right wire to thread through the holes of the beads you want to use. If you're not sure, bring your beads to a craft store, and try it out. If you get in the swing of things and start making lots and lots of projects, consider buying big spools of wire. It'll save you a bundle.

Beading Wire

Beading wire is an alternative to chain and perfect for stringing together lots of beads or other interesting finds. It's basically wire coated with nylon so it's nice and smooth. You'll be using crimps or crimp beads (see below) to secure your designs when you use beading wire. Beadalon is a common brand that you can find at your local craft store. Like jewelry wire, beading wire comes in different gauges, so make sure that your beads will fit. And just like jewelry wire, you can get discounts when you buy big spools of it.

Crimps/Crimp Beads

You can get these little beads in silver or gold. Once you string on beads or whatever finds you may want to add to your jewelry projects, you'll secure them by using your flat-nosed pliers to flatten the crimp bead to the wire.

Chain/Extender Chain

For most of the necklace and bracelet projects in this book, you can recycle old necklaces and bracelet chains that you already have. If you don't have any that you're willing to slice and dice, buy some extender or regular chain (you can buy it by the foot) at your local craft store or online. The great part about recycling a chain is that it already comes with the clasp on it. If you have to add your own clasp, just slide it on a jump ring and attach that to the last link in your chain.

Earring Hooks

The trick to making any earring project super easy. Available at any craft store in silver or gold, they have little loops at their base so that they're ready to attach beads to a jump ring, or have wire strung right through them.

Plain Headband/Tiara Bases

Simple metal headbands and tiaras (without any decoration) are available at most craft stores in silver and gold. If you have trouble finding tiara bases, you can take a headband base and bend it into a more circular shape. That should work just fine for your highness.

Brooch(es)

Just another word for pin. Vintage brooches are the key to making a lot of the projects in this book super fabulous.

WHERE TO LOOK

The first stop for finding material to make your jewelry: your place. Junk drawers, basements, garages, and attics are regular treasure troves. Tip: Tell your folks you want to help organize or clean up and you'll get some serious brownie points. Might come in handy when you want to ask if you can dissect those old necklaces you found in the attic or steal some of those random washers and nuts from the garage. Don't overlook your own jewelry box, either. There are probably a lot of things in there you haven't worn in forever. Consider recycling them and turning them into something you actually want to wear.

Lots of unexpected things can make for awesome bling. The list is endless, but here are some suggestions to get your gears turning: antique buttons, antique pearls, antique crystals, old chain, vintage earrings (clip-ons!), small charms, broken jewelry, washers, nuts, old keys, coins, silk flowers, vintage lace, sea glass, sea plastic, small pieces of driftwood, pebbles, shells.

Once you've exhausted options on the homefront, try some of these other places for hidden treasures.

Relatives
Let Aunt Esther and the rest of the gang know that you're making jewelry and would love to inherit old jewels, buttons, or anything else they might want to donate to a worthy cause (um, you). Don't turn things down just because they're ugly at first glance. You never know how you can reinvent them.

Beaches
Home to pieces of sea glass, driftwood, and colorful pieces of plastic. Bring a friend or parent and try venturing onto less populated or picturesque beaches where you're more likely to find treasures.

Garage/Yard Sales
When the weekend rolls around, you can usually find signs around the neighborhood advertising garage or yard sales. You know what they say about one person's trash being another's treasure—go to it!

Thrift Stores
Local thrift stores are a great place to find old chains, earrings, and other pieces of jewelry that you can recycle for new projects. Try the more out-of-the-way thrift stores. They'll be less picked over and probably have better prices.

Antique Malls/Shops
Chances are that someone in your family has dragged you to one of these at some point. You may have thought it was totally boring, but that's only because you didn't yet realize how you could put antique junk to use in your own jewelry projects. Keep an eye out for inexpensive chains, charms, and vintage brooches.

Sale Bins at Accessory Stores

Every mall has an accessory store or two, selling cheap jewelry and bejeweled thingamabobs for your hair. They usually have a sale bin chock-full of things that you wouldn't be caught dead wearing—but you can cut them up and use the beads and bling for projects of your own.

Recycle/Scrap Centers

Your town/city probably has a scrap or recycle center that is open to the public. It's the perfect place to find super cheap plastic bits and other random things.

Furniture Stores

Stores that sell leather sofas sometimes have old fabric swatches for sale or for free. These are a great source for good-quality leather.

Hardware Stores

Local hardware stores can be great places to find different styles of chains, which can be used for both bracelets and necklaces. Bonus: They're cheap, too!

Craft/Bead Stores

Check out the sale bins for beads and jewelry supplies. Even if these stores don't have the best prices, they're a great place to see beads and wire in person and compare colors, size, etcetera. If you've got a mom-and-pop type store, definitely pay a visit. The staff will probably be full of great advice and help and may be willing to offer you great discounts if you buy in bulk.

eBay

Good old eBay! This is a great resource, especially if you're looking for a specific color or type of bead, chain, etcetera. And remember the rules about bidding: Get permission from a parent, set a limit on how much you're willing to spend, and do it late in the game so that you don't push the price up too much.

Online Craft Suppliers

There are tons of bead websites out there and they're a great resource for finding deals on wire, beads, and other supplies. At the end of the book, you can find a useful list of websites that offer everything you need to make one-of-a-kind treasures. But if you've got a local mom-and-pop craft or jewelry supply store, check out prices there first. It's always good to support your local community, and you may get discounts on things if you just ask. Also: It never hurts to make friends with the folks who might be willing to help you sell your handmade jewelry!

VINTAGE GLAMOUR

RETRO-BAUBLE BRACELET

YOU WILL NEED:

- About 3 ft (1 m) of 0.8 mm wire
- Pliers
- A collection of antique beads
- A small lobster clasp

Chances are, your mom has a bunch of old jewelry somewhere in the back of a closet or drawer. Sure, most of it may be a little too vintage to wear as-is, but that doesn't mean it can't be repurposed to make something fabulous. Just a handful of Mom's old beads, any shape or size, can be transformed into an awesome, one-of-a-kind bracelet. And while she'd be a fool not to recognize how you've improved on the original, you might want to ask permission before getting all crafty with her classics.

1. Cut a 2 in. (5 cm) piece of wire (longer if you're using extra large beads).

2. Make a loop on one end by wrapping the wire back around itself a few times. Slide the bead onto the wire, using the loop as a stopper at the end.

3. To finish the beaded link, make a loop at the other end of the bead, cutting off any extra wire. You'll have two closed loops with a bead in the middle.

4. Repeat steps two and three with a new bead, but before closing up the end of your second loop, thread the wire through the loop of the original bead, linking the two loops together.

5. Keep adding beads to form a chain. Make it long enough to go around your wrist (longer if you want some of the beads to dangle from your wrist like charms).

6. Before closing the loop of the last bead on the bracelet, slip on a lobster clasp.

1.

2.

5.

CREATIVE TIP

REMIXED MEDIA

If rummaging through Mom's jewelry from ye olden times doesn't yield enough beads to make a full bracelet or necklace, you can use this same technique to make short beaded sections that you can combine with pieces of suede or ribbon for a funky, mixed-media look.

VINTAGE BRAIDED CHOKER

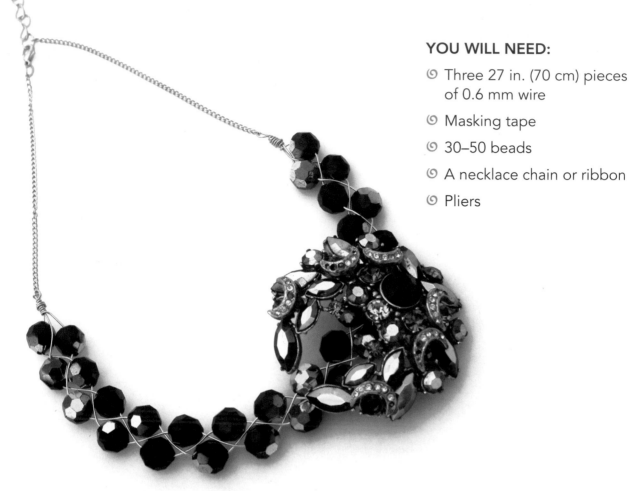

YOU WILL NEED:

- ⟲ Three 27 in. (70 cm) pieces of 0.6 mm wire
- ⟲ Masking tape
- ⟲ 30–50 beads
- ⟲ A necklace chain or ribbon
- ⟲ Pliers

This choker is the magical solution for those situations when you're stuck wearing something totally boring to a family wedding or school concert. And no, it's not magic in the get-you-out-of-having-to-go-to-that-boring-event kinda way, but we promise you'll have a better time with this beauty around your neck. For a sophisticated look, use beads that are roughly the same size and color (crystals or pearls = glamorous)—then you can attach an antique brooch as a centerpiece. Or, for funkier flair, mix and match different beads or stones.

1. Hold the three pieces of wire together with the pliers and use your fingers to wrap one of the wires around the other two about four times, leaving 1–1 1/2 in. (about 3–4 cm) of wire above the wrapping, so that you can make a loop at the end to attach the necklace chain later.

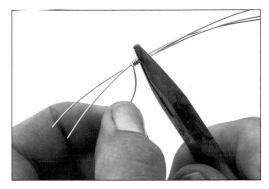

1.

2. Cut off the tail end of your wrapping wire and use masking tape to stick the bundle of wires to a table or tray, like you would when weaving a friendship bracelet. Now you're ready to start braiding.

3. Thread a bead onto the right-hand wire. In the same way that you would braid hair, cross the beaded wire over the middle wire so that it becomes the new middle wire..

4. Thread a bead onto the left-hand wire and cross it over the middle wire so that it becomes the new middle wire. The first few beads might be tricky to keep in place. They should sit at a slight diagonal from each other. When your cross your wires you want them tight enough to keep the beads from sliding around on the wires, but loose enough that they don't push the beads out of place. It might take a few tries to get the tension just right.

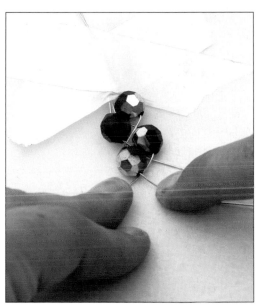

4.

5. Continue threading beads onto the side wires and braiding. Add a bead each time you cross a wire.

6. Stop braiding about 1 in. (3 cm) before the necklace is the right size for you. This gives you room to make a loop to attach to the necklace chain or ribbon. To finish off the necklace, braid the wires once more without adding any beads.

7.

7. To secure the end, wrap one wire around the other two just like you did at the beginning, then wrap one of the two remaining wires around the last one, leaving you with just one length of wire.

8. Cut your necklace chain at the middle point so you have two lengths of chain connected by the clasp. You might need to shorten the chains depending on how low you want the necklace to hang.

9. Start to bend the necklace's wire tail into a loop, thread it onto one end of the chain, and bend the loop closed by wrapping the wire back around itself. You can pinch it tightly with your pliers to make it more secure. Do the same on the other side of the necklace, attaching that wire tail to the necklace chain. If you want to fasten the necklace with ribbon instead, just thread your ribbon through the loops and tie a neat knot.

BLING RING

YOU WILL NEED:

- 3 ft (1 m) of 0.6 mm wire
- About 10 different sized beads
- A single centerpiece bead (or an old earring, small brooch, or vintage button)
- Pliers
- A file

Everybody needs a little bling sometimes. Whether it's for prom, or just to make a Tuesday a little more interesting, the Bling Ring is an easy way to take a beautiful bead, antique button, or earring, and turn it into a centerpiece sparkly enough to blind the paparazzi. Also: These babies make great presents.

1. Starting around 4 in. (10 cm) from one end, wrap the wire three times around the finger you'd like to wear the ring on (not too tight!). Pull it off your finger, holding the loops together.

2. Wrap the short tail end tightly around the loops three or four times to secure them, and cut off the tail end. This is now your ring band.

3. Choose one of your smaller beads and thread it onto the long piece of wire. Push it to the end toward the ring, then wrap the wire around the bead in a "C" shape to keep it in place. Wrap the wire once around the ring band to secure it.

4. Thread on another bead and secure it to the ring base in the same way. Keep adding your smaller beads using this technique, working in a roughly circular shape instead of in a line (like you would for a necklace). You may want to put your centerpiece bead or button on after about four or five beads, depending on their size.

1.

3.

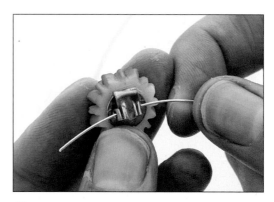

4b.

4c.

5. Work around your centerpiece, adding beads to frame it. Once you're satisfied with your design, squeeze it a little tighter and wrap the wire around the ring band again to secure it.

6. Tightly coil the wire around the whole ring band to make the ring stronger and more comfortable to wear.

7. When you've coiled the wire all the way around the ring band, wrap the end under your design and cut off any extra wire. Use pliers to bend the tail end into place and file it smooth so it doesn't poke your finger. Now, try it on. It may need some last minute reshaping, but otherwise, you're ready for the red carpet.

5.

6.

CREATIVE TIP

RING LEADER

You can use virtually anything for your ring's centerpiece—even if it doesn't have holes in it. Use the wire-wrapping technique in the Sea-Jewel Pendant project (page 38) to turn any souvenir into a bling-worthy centerpiece.

ROYAL JEWELS NECKLACE

YOU WILL NEED:
- ✪ A large vintage brooch
- ✪ 40–50 mixed beads
- ✪ 23 in. (60 cm) of beading wire
- ✪ 8 crimps
- ✪ A lobster clasp
- ✪ Extender chain
- ✪ A file
- ✪ Pliers

All the fun of looking like royalty without the hassle of running a kingdom. Just take an old brooch or pin (try grandma's jewelry box or a local flea market), a few beads, and *voilà*, you've got a gorgeous necklace that will transform strangers into loyal subjects in no time. This necklace looks especially regal when paired with a V-neck dress or shirt.

1. Cut the pin off the back of your brooch. The metal used in older brooches is usually soft, and it should come off fairly easily. If it's putting up more of a fight, just take your time and keep cutting around the base until it comes off. File down any sharp pieces of metal on the back of the brooch.

1.

2. Cut a 12 in. (30 cm) piece of wire and thread two crimps onto it. Then, thread the wire through one side of the brooch, pulling about 2 in. (5 cm) through.

3. Thread this small end back through the crimps to make a loop. Slide the crimps close to the brooch so that the loop is nice and tight around the brooch.

4. Use your pliers to firmly grip both crimps, pressing down hard to secure them to the wire. Cut off the tail end of the wire.

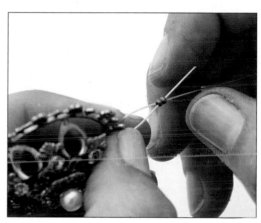

3.

5. Start threading your beads onto the wire. Don't be afraid to mix bead colors and styles. The randomness will make the design more interesting.

6. When you've threaded on enough beads to make half the length of your necklace, thread two crimps onto your wire. Loop your wire through the end of your extender chain and back down through the crimps, connecting the wire to the extender chain. Squeeze firmly with your pliers to secure the crimps to the wire. One side down, one more to go.

6a.

7. Thread the beads and crimps onto the other side of your necklace in the same way (this time looping the wire through a lobster clasp on the end instead of through the extender chain). Ta-da! Now you just need to practice that princess-ly wave.

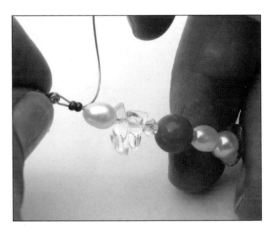

6b.

CREATIVE TIP

GO BIG

There's no such thing as "too much" when you're royalty. Choose a super big brooch and use two or three strands of beads on either side to make the necklace even more regal.

VINTAGE LACE CHOKER

YOU WILL NEED:

- A piece of vintage lace
- A few crystal beads or sequins
- 3 ft (1 m) of 0.6 mm wire
- A choker-length necklace (cut in the middle)
- Pliers
- A file
- Manicure/nail scissors
- White glue
- Water

Ever find a gorgeous vintage lace dress at a thrift store that you wished was in better condition so that you could actually wear it? The next best thing is buying that dress for super cheap and using some of that eye-catching lace for this project. Combining lace and beads makes for jewelry with great texture. Wear it to a fancy event, or, pair it with a leather jacket and jeans for an interesting contrast.

1. Mix 2–3 tablespoons of white glue with 2–3 tablespoons of water. Dip your lace into the mixture so that it's totally covered. Pull it out and set it to dry on a flat surface protected with plastic, like a plastic bag cut open.

2. Once the lace is dry, use nail scissors to cut the glue out of the open parts of the lace.

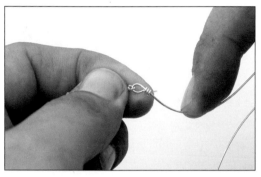

2.

3. Cut a 16 in. (40 cm) piece of wire and attach one end of it to your necklace chain by looping the wire through the last link in the chain, then wrapping the wire back around itself a few times.

4. Using your thumb and pointer finger, smooth the wire into a decorative curve. Thread a bead into the curve and wrap the wire around it in a "C" shape to keep it in place.

4.

5. Attach the lace to the wire by threading the wire through one end of the lace from front to back to front again, like you're sewing the lace with the wire.

5.

6. Make another curve in the wire at the front of the lace and thread on a bead, securing it with the wire "C" shape. Sew the wire through the lace again and add another bead to the wire. Continue using this technique until you reach the other end of the lace.

6.

7. Curve the wire at the end of the lace and thread on another bead, wrapping the wire around the bead in a "C" shape to keep it in place. Attach this end of the wire to the end of the necklace chain with a loop, the same way you did in step three.

8. Make your wirework as elaborate as you want. Just wrap a new wire around the loop, weave across the lace, and wrap the end around the other loop. When you're happy with your design, cut off the tail ends of the wires and file them down.

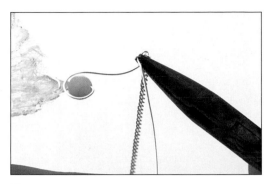

7.

CREATIVE TIP

EVERYDAY CORSAGE
You can use this design to make a wrist corsage–inspired bracelet. Just use a slightly larger piece of lace and bend the wire so that the shape fits around your wrist. For an edgier look, use black lace.

8a.

8b.

8c.

BEACH
FINDS

SEA-JEWEL PENDANT

YOU WILL NEED:

- A stone or pebble (one with a flat shape works best)
- 3 ft (1 m) of 0.6 mm wire
- A chain, ribbon, or piece of leather to string the pendant on
- Pliers

Who needs diamonds and rubies when the ocean spits out gorgeous (and free!) gems all the time? This pendant is a simple and classy way to turn a beach-trip souvenir into an everyday necklace. Also: Once you master this wire-wrapping technique, you'll be ready to turn anything (well, almost anything ... we don't recommend fruits, vegetables, or family pets) into a stunning piece of jewelry.

1. Starting about 2 in. (5 cm) from one end of the wire, hold the pebble or glass with your fingers and firmly bend the wire around the top corner.

2. Wrap the wire all the way around the width of the glass. Keep the tension as tight as you can and try not to let the wire slip.

3. Wrap the wire two more times around the width of the glass, then take it to the bottom and wrap it once vertically around the glass, over the three horizontal wraps.

4. Take the wire back to the top of the glass and twist it together with the 2 in. (5 cm) end you left at the back.

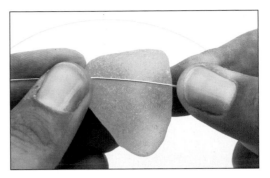

1.

3a.

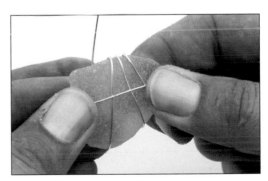

3b.

5. Thread the longer wire end back underneath the three widthwise wires, and bring it back up to the top of the pendant. Wrap it around the twist at the top to make the twist more secure.

6. Cut off this long end and make a loop with the 2 in. (5 cm) wire, wrapping the wire back around itself a few times to secure it. Cut off any remaining wire tails. You can wear it on a chain as a pendant, or use it as a charm on a bracelet.

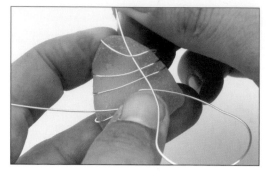

5a.

5b.

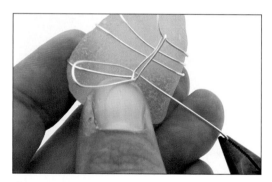

6a.

6b.

CREATIVE TIP

BE(MORE)JEWELED

If you've got a whole collection of sea glass pieces, you can string them together end-to-end to create a necklace or bracelet. Just use the longer piece of wire to make a loop at the other end of each piece of glass. Connect them with jump rings. And there you have it: jewels befitting a mermaid.

COLORFUL RECYCLED NECKLACE

YOU WILL NEED:

- 3–5 pieces of weathered sea-plastic, about 2–4 in. (5–10 cm) long
- Beading wire
- About 20 crimps
- A Dremel tool or hand drill
- A mix of chunky vintage beads and semiprecious stones
- Pliers

Did you know that there's a floating island in the ocean twice the size of Texas made of nothing but discarded plastic? Here's an awesome project that is both good for the environment and your style. All kinds of sea-polished plastic washes ashore, and it's usually brightly colored and interestingly shaped: the perfect material for a bold piece of jewelry. Mix the plastic in with chunky vintage beads or semiprecious stones, pair it with a gauzy tank top, and you get a look that's equal parts summery and modern.

1. Get your plastic pieces ready by drilling a small hole in each end of each piece.

2. Take an 8 in. (20 cm) piece of beading wire and thread two small crimps onto it. Then thread it through one of the drilled holes in a piece of plastic.

3. Bend the beading wire back about 1 in. (3 cm) from the end and thread it back through the two crimps to make a loop. Using your pliers, squeeze the crimps firmly to secure them to the beading wire, and trim off the end of the short wire. Your piece of plastic should be hanging from your beading wire by a loop.

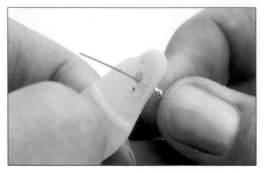

2.

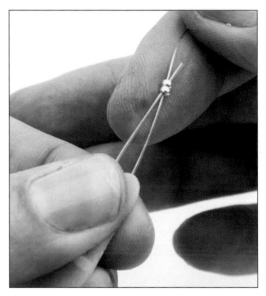

3a.

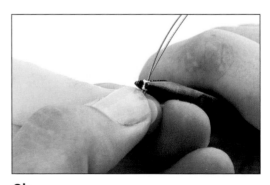

3b.

CREATIVE TIP

LOOK SHARP(IE)
If your plastic isn't as colorful as you'd like, or if you want to make your necklace even more unique, you can use colored Sharpie markers to draw patters and designs right on the plastic. Try using patterns based on ocean life, like brain coral (looks just like how it sounds), great star coral (clusters of little sun shapes), or the patterns of the waves.

4. Thread a mix of beads onto your beading wire, leaving yourself about 2 in. (5 cm) of wire at the end so you can attach another piece of sea plastic. You don't have to cover the whole length of wire in beads if you don't like that look. Trust your eye and keep in mind how long you want the finished necklace to be.

4.

5. On the remaining 2 in. (5 cm) of wire, add another piece of plastic to the necklace using the loop and crimp technique from step three. Cut another piece of beading wire to attach through the other hole in this second piece of plastic and thread a mix of beads onto that wire.

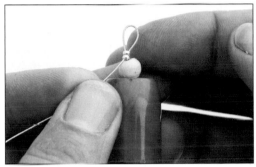

5.

6. Continue adding plastic and beads to the necklace using this technique until it's the right length. To finish the necklace, just loop and crimp a final piece of beading wire through the hole in the other end of the first piece of plastic you started your necklace with, making it one continuous circle.

OCEAN'S CHARM BRACELET

YOU WILL NEED:

- A bracelet with large enough links to add charms
- Small finds from the beach such as shells, sea plastic, and sea glass
- About 10 bright glass beads or semiprecious stones
- 3 ft (1 m) of 0.6 mm wire
- About 10 medium-sized jump rings
- Pliers
- A file
- A Dremel tool or hand drill (optional)

So you're always stuffing your pockets with strange colorful things you find at the beach. *What's with all that junk you keep picking up?* people ask skeptically. Ha! What these folks don't understand is that that "junk" is actually the perfect material for some awesome wearable art. Some ocean charms and a bracelet are pretty much all you need to make this beauty. Try local flea markets and garage sales for an old bracelet. You need a chain with links that are large enough to add charms to using jump rings. Or, cut up an old necklace and transform it into a bracelet. Happy beachcombing.

1. Lay your bracelet out on your work surface to plan your design. First, decide where you want to place your main beach finds and attach them to the bracelet with jump rings. If your finds don't already have holes in them, you can wrap them in wire (see the Sea-Jewel Pendant on page 38) or you can drill small holes in them with a Dremel tool or hand drill and attach them to the bracelet with jump rings.

1a.

2. To prepare your bead charms, make a spiral ending (see the Elegant First-Date Earrings on page 58) on a length of wire about 3 in. (8 cm) long. Thread on your chosen bead and attach it to the bracelet by bending the wire back at 90 degrees to start to make a loop. Thread the bent end of the wire through the chain and wrap the wire back around itself a few times to finish the loop. Cut off any tail ends.

1b.

3. Check the fit and look of the bracelet by trying it on. You might see some gaps in the design when you do this and decide to add a few more charms.

2.

4. Once you're happy with the design, run your fingers over your bracelet to check that there aren't any sharp wire ends sticking out. If there are, squeeze them into place with your pliers and file them down. And there you have it: a lovely, dangly, vacation-souvenir bracelet.

4.

FISHING-NET CUFF

YOU WILL NEED:

- A long piece of fishing net–like cotton twine
- 20–30 small beach finds (shells, sea plastic, or glass)
- About 5–6 big, bright round beads (pearls look great, too)
- About 6 ft (2 m) of 0.4 mm wire
- 1 in. (3 cm) of 0.8 mm wire
- Pliers
- A crochet hook

When there are still waaaaay too many months to go until vacation, you can feast your eyes on this fishing-net–inspired cuff and daydream about all the fun you're sure to catch come summer. Raid your supply of beach finds from last summer, or just use colorful glass and plastic beads that remind you of vacation times. If you've never crocheted before, you might need to look up some instructional videos online. It's totally worth taking a few minutes to learn the basics: Once you get the hang of it, it's an awesome and simple way to make all kinds of jewelry, hats, scarves, and more.

1. Get a long piece of twine and make a loop at one end by loosely double knotting it around your finger. Slide the loop off your finger.

2. Put your crochet hook through this loop from front to back. Wrap the twine once in a clockwise direction around your hook above the original loop. Using the hook, pull the twine toward the loop while pushing the loop off the hook, over the twine. Now you have two loops joined.

3. Continue crocheting so that you make a chain. If you're just learning how to crochet and it's a little confusing, look up demonstration videos online to help you learn. (Tip: Keep your crochet work loose with biggish loops. Don't worry if it looks a little messy. That's part of the charm of the design.)

4. Once the cuff is just long enough to fit around your wrist, pull the twine through the last loop to end it and keep it from unraveling.

1.

2.

3.

5. Now you're ready to attach your beach finds. Cut a 3 ft (1 m) piece of 0.4 mm wire and wrap one end tightly around the end of your twine chain four times to secure it.

6. Thread your beads and beach finds onto the wire. Make a little loop at the unattached end by wrapping the wire back around itself a few times, to keep the beads from falling off.

7. Slide all your beach finds to the end of the wire that's attached to the twine. Put your crochet hook through the first twine link from front to back. Wrap the wire clockwise around the hook and pull it through, pushing the twine off the hook. You should have a wire loop attached to your twine chain.

5.

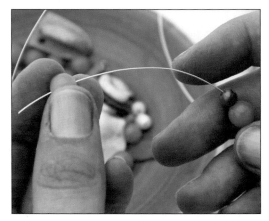

6.

7.

CREATIVE TIP

CATCH OF THE DAY
If you're having too much fun crocheting and daydreaming about the summertime, why stop? You can make a bib necklace to match your cuff. Just crochet another, similarly sized piece, bend it into a crescent moon shape and use jump rings to attach ribbon or necklace chain to each side.

8. Keeping the wire loop on the hook, put the hook through the next twine link. Push the first beach find right up next to the hook, then wrap the wire clockwise around the hook. Pull that wire through the first wire loop on the hook, then through the twine loop. Only the new wire loop should be left on the hook.

8.

9. Keep going with this technique, crocheting the wire and beads to the twine chain. Don't worry if it looks messy; it's supposed to look sea-weathered. Adapt your design in any way you want: For a funkier cuff, add on another piece of beaded wire and crochet back down the twine. For a more silver-y cuff, crochet another beaded wire onto your wire strand.

10a.

10. Once you're done crocheting, pull the end of the wire through the last chain link like you did when you tied off the twine. Then gently bend your cuff into an oval shape with your fingers.

10b.

11. To secure your cuff, make a hook out of 1 in. (3 cm) of 0.8 mm wire. Bend the wire into a hook with your fingers and use the pliers to make a small loop at the end so the wire doesn't scratch you. Attach the hook to one end of your cuff by looping it through the twine and wrapping the wire back around itself a few times. Your hook can grab onto any link in your twine chain.

11.

SEA-JEWEL CUFF

YOU WILL NEED:

- ☉ About 10 ft (3 m) of 0.4 mm wire
- ☉ 4 in. (10 cm) of 0.8 mm wire
- ☉ 40–50 stones or beads (clear crystal beads and pearls work well)
- ☉ 5–6 pieces of wire-wrapped sea glass (see Sea-Jewel Pendant on page 38)
- ☉ Pliers
- ☉ A crochet hook

What happens when you take a pirate's buried treasure, mix it with the magical light of the sun setting behind the sea and add a dash of mermaid magic? We're not entirely sure, but we think you'd get the Sea-Jewel Cuff. It's like the Fishing-Net Cuff, but fancier. Wear this when you're ready for an evening full of unexpected magic.

1. Take a long piece of 0.4 mm wire and make a loop at one end by wrapping the wire back around itself a few times.

2. Put your crochet hook through this loop from front to back. Wrap the wire once in a clockwise direction around your hook above the original loop. Using the hook, pull the wire toward the loop while pushing the loop off the hook, over the wire. Now you have two loops joined.

3. Continue crocheting the wire into a chain. Once the chain is long enough to wrap comfortably around your wrist, slide the last loop off your hook and push the wire end through it from front to back to pull it into a knot and keep your chain from unraveling. (Tip: Keep your crochet work loose with biggish loops. Don't worry if it looks a little messy. That's part of the charm of this cuff.)

4. Now you're ready to attach your glass and beads. Cut a 3 ft (1 m) piece of 0.4 mm wire and wrap one end tightly around the end of your cuff base four times to secure it.

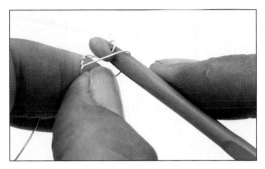

2a.

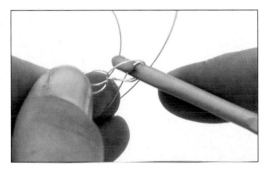

2b.

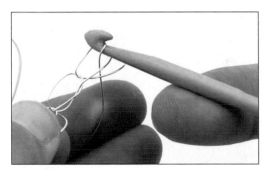

3a.

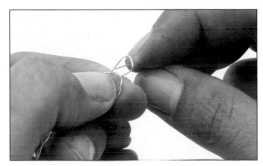

3b.

5. Thread your beads and a couple of wrapped sea-glass pieces onto the wire. Make a little loop at the unattached end by wrapping the wire back around itself a few times, to keep the beads and seaglass from falling off.

6. Crochet this beaded wire to the wire cuff (use the technique from the Fishing-Net Cuff on page 46). To make a wide cuff, add another 3 ft. (1 m) of 0.4 mm wire, threaded with beads and sea-glass, and crochet it to the cuff. Keep adding extra rows until the cuff is as wide as you want it to be.

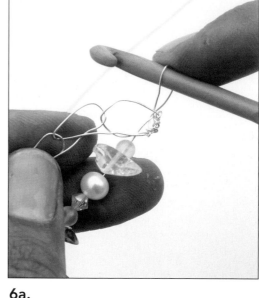

6a.

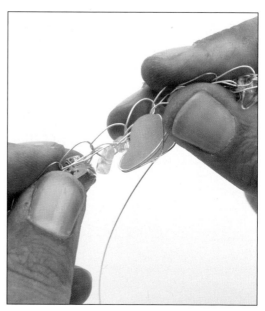

6b.

CREATIVE TIP

THE SEA-NECK ROUTE
For a sea-inspired showstopper, make a choker by crocheting a piece that's long enough to go around your neck. It'll catch the light in all kinds of amazing ways and make you feel like you're on a beautiful island, your toes dug into some warm, white sand.

7. Once you've reached the end of the cuff, wrap the end of the wire around the final chain loops a few times and cut off the wire tail end. Then gently bend your cuff into an oval shape with your fingers.

8. To secure your cuff, make a hook out of 4 in. (10 cm) of 0.8 mm wire. Bend the wire into a hook with your fingers and use the pliers to make a small loop at the end so the wire doesn't scratch you. Attach the hook to one end of your cuff by looping it through the wire chain and wrapping the wire back around itself a few times. Your hook can grab onto any link in your cuff.

7.

8.

SIXTIES STRING-ART NECKLACE

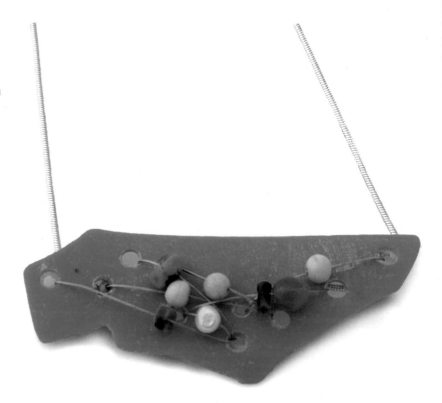

YOU WILL NEED:

- A medium/large piece of sea plastic
- 3 ft. (1 m) of beading wire
- 2 crimps
- A few small bright beads/ stones
- A Dremel tool or hand drill
- Pliers
- A file
- A chain, ribbon, or piece of leather to string the pendant on
- Jump rings (optional)

Part of an artistic style that was popularized in the sixties and seventies, string art is all about taking string and weaving it into geometric or abstract designs. With a little recycled plastic and a few colorful beads, you can create a funky string-art-style necklace that'd make Andy Warhol proud.

CREATIVE TIP

STRING IT ALONG
You can use a few of these string-art pieces to make a Colorful Recycled Necklace project (page 41) even more eye-catching. Or, use jump rings to link together enough string-art sections to go around your wrist for a sixties-inspired bracelet.

1. Drill random holes in your piece of plastic; cluster some together and leave spaces of plastic without holes. Then, use your file to sand down the surface of the plastic so it doesn't feel sharp.

2. Cut a 16 in. (40 cm) piece of beading wire, thread a crimp onto one end, and use pliers to squeeze it into place about 0.5 mm from the end of the wire.

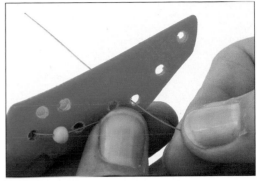

3.

3. Thread a bead onto the wire. Then thread the long end of the wire through the plastic from back to front so that the crimp and bead act as stoppers to keep the beading wire from pulling all the way through the hole. Thread a small bead onto the wire at the front of the plastic, then thread the wire through a diagonally positioned hole. Pull the wire tight to hold the bead close to the plastic.

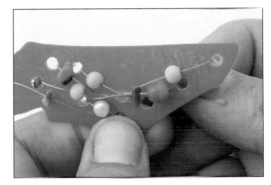

4.

4. From the back, send the wire through another hole to the front. Place another bead on the wire, thread it though another hole, and repeat until all the holes are beaded through. Use the same holes multiple times. It looks good if the wires cross each other.

5.

5. When you're satisfied with the design, thread the beading wire through one last hole to the back of the plastic. Thread a crimp onto the beading wire and push it up against the plastic. Secure the crimp to the wire by squeezing it with your pliers. Make sure the crimp won't slip back through the hole to the front of the plastic before cutting off the tail end of the wire.

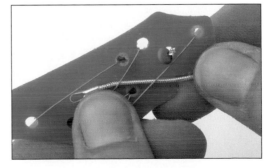

6.

6. Thread a chain, ribbon, or piece of leather through the wire at the back of the plastic. If the wire is too tight in the back, attach large jump rings to wires on either end of the back of the plastic, and thread your chain through there.

USE WHAT
YOU HAVE

ELEGANT FIRST-DATE EARRINGS

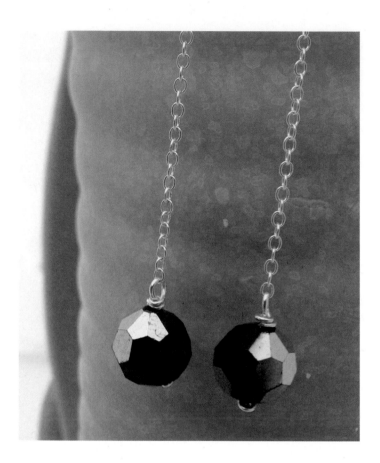

YOU WILL NEED:

- Two sophisticated beads (Hint: Vintage crystal/pearl or glass beads rescued from an old necklace work well.)

- About 4 in. (10 cm) of chain (the kind used for necklaces). Make sure the chain has large enough links to thread wire through

- 6 in. (15 cm) of 0.6 mm wire (0.4 mm if the bead holes are very small)

- Two earring hooks

- Round-nose pliers and scissors

So you're finally going out with that someone you've had your eye on for weeks (okay, maybe months). You want to look good, but not like you're trying too hard. These elegant earrings can put the finishing touch on a wide range of looks—from a summer dress to a sweater and jeans. They're classic and versatile, which means you can wear them just about anywhere, and you don't have to worry that they'll go out of style next week. They're also super easy to make: Just find a couple of sophisticated beads that will catch the light and entrance your date, then follow the directions.

1. Cut two 3 in. (8 cm) pieces of wire. Make a small spiral at one end of each wire by gripping the end of the wire with the the pliers and wrapping the wire around the tip of the pliers twice. Bend the wire at a 90-degree angle so that the spiral sits at the bottom of it like a ledge. Thread a bead onto each wire so it sits on top of the spiral.

1.

2. Cut two 1–2 in. (3–5 cm) pieces of chain. Make them longer if you want your earrings to be more dramatic.

3. Thread the end of one of the beaded wires through the last link in one of the chains, bend it down toward the bead to make a little loop, and wrap the wire back around itself a few times to secure the loop. Cut off any excess wire. Repeat this step for the other earring.

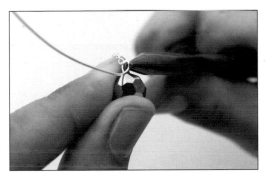

3.

4. Bend open the loop at the base of each earring hook and slide the top link of each chain into the loops. Then, bend both loops closed.

4.

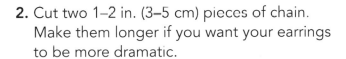

CREATIVE TIP

CREATE A CLUSTER

If your date is more about rocking out at a concert than eating fancy food and watching a foreign film, make your earrings more casual (in a retro punk rock kinda way) by creating a clustered look. To do this, simply attach additional beaded chains to your earring hooks. *Voilà*: Instant edge.

ART NOUVEAU PENDANT

YOU WILL NEED:

- A stone or pebble (one with a flat shape works best)

- 3 ft (1 m) of 0.6 mm wire

- A chain, ribbon, or piece of leather to string the pendant on

- A small stone, pearl, or bead to hang from the pendant

- Pliers

Art Nouveau is a style that emerged in the early 1900s, and it was all about the idea that everything that surrounds us, from furniture to jewelry, should be beautiful works of art. This pendant is the perfect example: Start with an ordinary rock or pebble, and you end up with a beautiful pendant that is elegant enough to wear to a fancy dinner, but simple enough to wear with jeans and a T-shirt. Bonus: You can use this wire-wrapping technique to turn any everyday object into a gorgeous pendant.

1. Cut a 20 in. (50 cm) piece of wire and start wrapping your stone. Wrap around the edges, making a tight cage for your stone, until you have about a 2 in. (5 cm) tail of wire sticking upward.

2. Wrap that wire over and under the wire wrapped at the top of the stone a few times to make it more secure.

3. Cut a new piece of wire and, starting at the top of the stone, wrap the stone in the opposite direction. Finish by wrapping the tail end of that wire around the first tail end. Wrap one more wire around your stone, this time starting at the bottom. Make sure this wire's tail is at the bottom of your stone, and make a loop in that tail by wrapping the wire back around itself a few times. This is where your pendant drop will hang.

4. Smooth and shape the wires in any way you choose. You might want to pull them apart more or squeeze them closer together. Whatever kind of design you choose, just make sure your stone stays put.

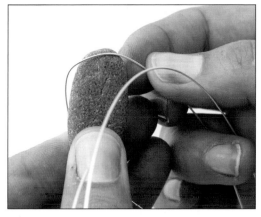

1.

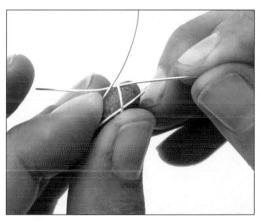

2.

3.

5. Get your pendant drop ready by making a small spiral ending on a 2 in. (5 cm) piece of wire (see the Elegant First-Date Earrings on page 58). Thread your bead onto the wire and attach it to the loop at the bottom of your stone by threading the wire through the loop and back around itself a few times to secure it.

6. Make a loop in the wire at the top of the stone by wrapping the wire back around itself a few times and cutting off any tail ends. File down any sharp ends in the wire and hang your pendant on a chain, ribbon, or piece of leather.

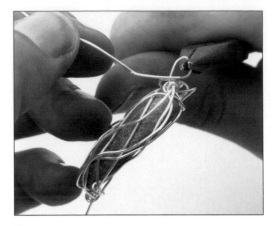

5a.

5b.

CREATIVE TIP

GO LONG

For a more dramatic look, you can create a longer, three-tiered nouveau pendant. Just wrap another, smaller rock or pebble and attach it below the larger one with a jump ring. Then attach your small bead or pearl to this second, smaller stone.

JEWELED BRANCHES NECKLACE

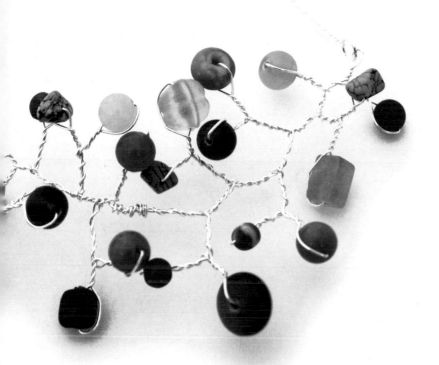

YOU WILL NEED:

- About 3 ft (1 m) of 0.6 mm wire
- A mix of roughly 20 small beads, buttons, or sequins
- A necklace chain, leather, or ribbon
- Two jump rings
- Pliers

Remember that feeling you used to get when you were a kid, staring up at the branches of a tree, watching the sun illuminate its leaves? The Jeweled Branches Necklace is an unusual design inspired by Mother Nature that'll recapture that feeling. Mix and match different sized and colored beads. Or, for a more dressy look, stick to pearl and crystal beads or variations of one color.

1. Cut a 20 in. (50 cm) piece of wire and find the middle point by gently folding it in half. Using your pliers to hold the wire at this midpoint, twist the wires together with your fingers for about a 1/2 in. (1–2 cm), leaving a loop at the top where your pliers are.

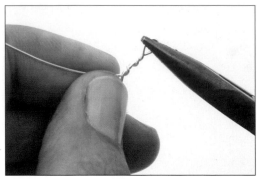

1.

2. Choose the first bead (or button or sequin) and thread it onto one of the wire ends. At the point where you'd like the bead to stick out and become its own branch, fold the wire, holding the bead at the top of the fold. Gently hold the bead in place with your pliers and start twisting the wires together like you did in step one. Twist them until they meet the point where your first branch started. Then twist the wires from both branches together for about 1/4 in. (1/2 cm).

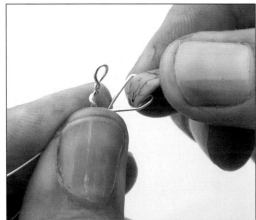

2a.

CREATIVE TIP

BRANCH OUT

If you want the design to be a little bigger (like in the photo), you can make another piece in the same way and then twist them together in the middle. Or, go crazy and make enough branching pieces to join into an amazing piece that you can wear as a bracelet.

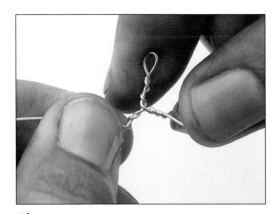

2b.

3. Next, put a bead on the other wire end and twist it in place, just like you did with the first one. Twist to the point where the branches meet, then twist the two long pieces together for about 1/2 in. (1 cm). Don't worry if it doesn't look perfect. The design is meant to be quirky and unique. Just remember to keep twisting the wires together to create a main branch after adding your beads.

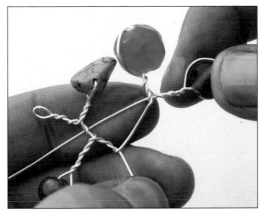

3.

4. When your wire starts to run out, you should have a design that's about 3 in. (8 cm) long. To finish the necklace, make an end loop and wrap the wire around itself a few times to secure it. Cut off the tail end of the wire. You can attach a chain with jump rings to the loops at the ends of your design, or thread a leather piece or ribbon through the loops and tie it in a knot.

4a.

4b.

NEWSSTAND NECKLACE

YOU WILL NEED:

- Colorful old magazine pages
- Clear-drying craft glue
- A pencil
- A medium-size paintbrush
- Some cord, leather, or thin ribbon
- Colorful and chunky beads

If you've got old magazines lying around, you almost have everything you need to make some truly unique beads. If you're looking for a gift idea that's as easy on the eyes as it is on the environment and your wallet, this project is the clear winner. People used to make paper beads like these back in the 20s and 30s, and they have an awesome vintage flair that you can customize by choosing magazine pages that are just the right color combinations for your artistic vision.

CREATIVE TIP

EXTRA! EXTRA!
Because these beads are made out of paper, they're super light so it's comfortable to wear a really long strand of them. Consider making a necklace long enough to wrap around your neck three or four times for a cool layered look.

1. Cut some long strips of magazine, slightly tapered at one end like long triangles. Each strip will become a bead.

2. Wrap the fat end of the strip tightly around the pencil, then use the paintbrush to spread a thin layer of glue from the fat end of the strip to the narrow end. Remember: The side you glue will be the inside of the bead, so keep your favorite side facing out. Tightly roll the strip around the pencil. You may need to put a little more glue on the end to seal the bead.

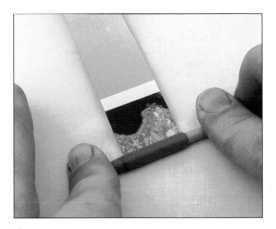

2a.

3. Take the bead off the pencil and thread it onto some twine. Paint the outside of the bead with a thick layer of glue to seal it and then hang it up to dry.

4. Use this technique to make as many beads as you like, then leave them to dry on the twine overnight.

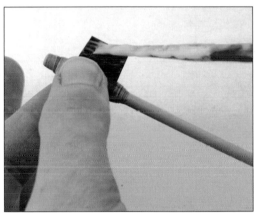

2b.

5. Choose some other beads that coordinate well with your paper beads: Chunky stones, vintage plastic, and wooden beads echo the DIY theme.

6. Cut a long piece of cord, suede, or ribbon and start threading on the paper and other beads. You can either leave them free to move or separate them with knots. Once you have enough beads on your cord, tie the ends of the cord together to make the necklace your preferred length. If the necklace doesn't fit over your head, make sure the knot is easy to untie and re-tie.

TOOLBOX BRACELET

YOU WILL NEED:

- ◎ A bracelet-length piece of chain with large enough links to add charms
- ◎ 0.6 mm and 0.8 mm wire
- ◎ Small odds and ends from a toolbox or hardware store (old washers, bolts, unidentifiable plastic objects, etc.)
- ◎ Pliers
- ◎ About 10 chunky jump rings
- ◎ A few medium-size round beads
- ◎ A file
- ◎ A lobster clasp

Love all those random doodads at the hardware store? Then this bracelet is for you. A multi-sensory delight, not only does this baby look super cool, it makes a delightful tinkling sound whenever you move your hand. Another bonus: The more stuff you add to charm bracelets, the better they look, so you can keep adding random charms to it whenever the mood strikes. The next time you're bored on a rainy Sunday, you'll know just what to do. And before you hit up the hardware store, check that old toolbox gathering dust in the garage. You may find a treasure trove right at home.

1. Lay your chain out on your work surface and place the toolbox charms roughly where you want them to go.

2. Sort out the charms that can be easily attached with jump rings, such as washers and nuts, and attach them to the bracelet with the jump rings.

3. For the other toolbox charms and beads that can't be attached to the bracelet with jump rings, wrap them in wire (see the Sea-Jewel Pendant on page 38) or thread them onto a piece of wire (see the Elegant First-Date Earrings on page 58) and attach them to the bracelet.

4. Attach a lobster clasp to one end of the bracelet chain and loop it through the other end of the chain for a bracelet closure.

5. Run your fingers over the bracelet to check for sharp ends sticking out. If you find any, squeeze them into place with your pliers or gently file them down.

3.

CREATIVE TIP

TOOLBOX TOOLBELT

For a super tough look, make a toolbox belt. Go to your local hardware store, and buy a length of chain long enough to go around your waist. Consider using thicker 1 mm wire to attach your charms. Bonus: With all those useful pieces of hardware hanging around your waist, you'll be able to fix nearly anything on the fly.

CUSTOMIZED CUFF

YOU WILL NEED:

- A piece of leather or suede that fits around your wrist
- A large sew-on snap
- 3 ft (1 m) of embroidery thread
- A few stones or beads to accompany your string design
- A large needle
- Sharp scissors
- A pen

Remember that leather skirt you bought last year because you had to have it and then wore it exactly once? This project is the perfect crafty solution. All you need is some old leather or suede and some imagination. Experiment by cutting cuffs of different widths, and sewing different patterns—from geometric and abstract designs to words. Because you can make about thirty unique cuffs from just one old leather skirt, they're the perfect gift idea.

CREATIVE TIP

CHANGE IT TO A CHOKER

It's just as easy to make a choker as a cuff. Cut a width and length of leather or suede that feels comfortable around your neck and get to working your design magic with a needle and thread. If designs with thread don't suit your fancy, just stick to sewing beads onto your cuff or choker.

1. Trim the leather with scissors to shape your cuff. A rectangle works well, but you can cut it into any shape you like. When you wrap it around your wrist, it must be long enough for the ends to overlap comfortably. Later you'll sew the snap onto the overlapping ends.

2. Wrap the leather around your wrist and find the center, where you'll start drawing your design.

3. A great design option is string art. Using straight lines, create beautiful patterns (like the parabola in the picture). For inspiration, search online for "string art patterns." Once you draw a design onto the leather, you're ready to sew over it.

4. Tread a 16 in. (40 cm) piece of embroidery thread onto your needle. Tie a double knot in the loose end of the thread so the thread won't pull through the cuff when you're sewing. If you want your design to really pop, choose a color that contrasts sharply with the color of your cuff.

5. Stick your needle through the cuff from back to front and start tracing your design with the thread. Once you're finished, tie the thread off on the back of your cuff.

6. To add more texture, sew beads or stones onto your cuff. Bring your needle through the cuff from back to front, thread on your bead, and secure it by looping through the bead with a few more stitches. Tie the thread off on the back of your cuff.

7. When you've finished all the designs on your cuff, sew on the snap. Use enough stitches to sew on each half of the snap securely, and make sure they line up when you bring the two ends of your cuff around your wrist. Done!

5.

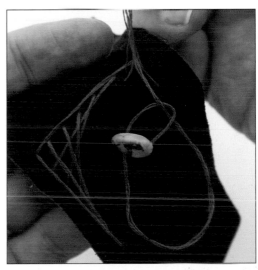

6.

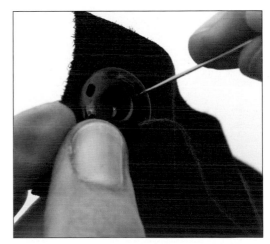

7.

JULIET TIARA

YOU WILL NEED:

- 2 green branches 20–23 in. (50–60 cm)—long and thin enough so that you can bend them
- 6 ft (2 m) each of 0.4 mm and 0.6 mm wire
- A few pearl and sparkly crystal beads
- Pliers
- A file
- Superglue (optional)

O, Romeo, Romeo! Wherefore art thou Romeo? **This is the perfect accessory for the hopeless romantic who can't stop reading Charlotte Brontë or Shakespeare. With just a couple of twigs, a little wire, and some sparkly beads, you'll be transformed into an ethereal maiden. Wear it to prom with a long, flowing dress, and you're sure to turn Romeo's head.**

1. Remove the leaves from your branches and bend the branches into a horseshoe shape.

1.

2. Bind the two branches together on one end by wrapping a piece of 0.6 mm wire around them five or six times. Make a small loop in the wire by wrapping it back around itself; cut off any excess wire. You'll use the loop to attach your tiara to your hair with bobby pins later.

2.

3. Wind the branches around each other a few times and then bind them together at the other end with a 20 in. (50 cm) piece of 0.6 mm wire. Make a loop in that wire just like you did with the first one, but don't cut off the extra wire. Keep it attached for the next step.

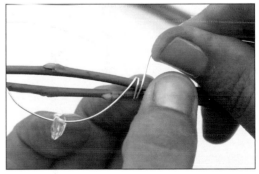

4. Bend that same piece of wire into a small hill shape above the branches, thread on a pearl, and wrap the wire once around the tiara base to secure it.

4.

CREATIVE TIP

FLOWERS IN YOUR HAIR
If you want an even more romantic look, you can slide the stems of fresh flowers into the wirework. If you're using larger flowers, you may need to secure the stems to the tiara by winding some extra wire around them.

5. Now bend that wire into a hill shape below the branches, thread on a crystal bead, and wrap it around the tiara base to secure it. Continue using this technique until you reach the other end of your branches. Wrap the wire around the end of the branches a few times to secure it.

6. Weave your way back across the branches, using the same technique you did before, only this time use a 20 in. (50 cm) piece of 0.4 mm wire. To get a more organic, wood nymph–like look, try to secure the wire to the branches in between the other hill shapes so it cuts across them. When you reach the other end of the branches, wrap the wire around them a few times to secure it.

7. Loosely wrap the two ends of your branches together with some extra wire and leave them to dry into the right shape overnight. If you want your beads and pearls to stay in place, use a drop of superglue to secure them to the wire.

8. Once the tiara is dry, remove the wire connecting the two ends. Tuck any sharp ends in place with the pliers and file them down if you need to. Bobby pin your tiara to your hair using the little loops at each end. Breathtaking!

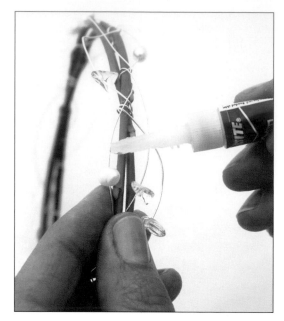

7a.

7b.

SO-QUIRKY-IT'S-COOL NECKLACE

YOU WILL NEED:

- A few little kitschy charms (quirky earrings, old charms, odd little buttons, brooches)
- Some old necklace chain to cut up
- 10–14 gold-plated jump rings (including two large, decorative ones)
- Pliers
- Beading wire (optional)

Everyone's got a special place in their hearts for quirky charms. From an old Girl Scouts pin to that pocket-sized Eiffel Tower replica your mom brought back from a business trip, this project is a great opportunity to use up any random doodads you might have lying around. Don't be afraid to embrace your goofy side.

1. If you're starting with a complete necklace chain, find the middle and cut it twice, about 1 in. (3 cm) from either side of the midpoint, leaving you with two long chains connected by the clasp and one 2 in. (5 cm) chain. Find another piece of chain about 3 in (8 cm) long to add later.

2. On both ends of the main necklace chain use small jump rings to attach your larger, decorative jump rings.

3. Now you're ready to attach the two smaller pieces of chain to the main necklace. Bend open a jump ring and slide one end of each small chain onto it. Attach this jump ring to the larger, decorative jump ring. Do the same on the other side, completing the circle of your necklace.

4. Cut some varying lengths of chain to hang from your decorative jump rings like tassels. You don't have to hang the same amount of tassels or charms from both decorative jump rings. The more asymmetrical your necklace is, the quirkier it will look. Attach these chain lengths to the jump ring the same way you did in step three.

2.

3–4.

5. Get your charms ready to attach. Hook them onto jump rings if possible, or thread them onto some wire with a spiral loop at one end (see the technique in the Elegant First-Date Earrings project on page 58). If you're using a small brooch, you might have to take off the pin backing (see the technique in the Royal Jewels Necklace project on page 30).

5.

6. Lay out your necklace and charms to plan their placement and then attach them to the extra dangling chains or decorative jump rings with the small jump rings or wire. Is your name Zooey Deschanel? Because you look so quirky and cool.

6.

CREATIVE TIP

BELT IT OUT

Admit it: You've got more kitsch than you thought. A lot more. Well, you're in luck: Just collect enough chain to thread through your belt loops and you can create a quirk-tastic belt. For extra flair, and a delightful clinking sound whenever you swish your hips, attach short tassels of chain all around your belt.

DIVA
DESIGNS

BILLIE HOLIDAY HEADBAND

YOU WILL NEED:

- Some artificial flowers (a cluster of medium-sized flowers, one large flower, and 6–7 small flowers make a good combination)
- A plain silver headband
- 3 ft (1 m) each of 0.6 mm and 0.4 mm wire
- About 20 sparkly crystal beads and some sequins
- Pliers
- Scissors
- A file
- A needle

A tribute to the jazz great Billie Holiday (aka Lady Day) who often wore white gardenias in her hair, this headband will channel your inner songstress. For a more casual look, use smaller flowers. But if you're looking to make a statement, go big and bright. And don't be surprised if you're suddenly in the mood to croon some love songs.

The Large Flowers (steps 1–3)

1. Find a cluster of flowers to feature on your headband, and wrap the stems together with the 0.6 mm wire as close as you can to the base of the flowers. Leave a longish wire tail to attach the flowers to the headband base. Cut the flower stems off right below your wire wrapping.

2. Find one larger flower you'd also like to add to your design. Cut the flower from it's stem and use a needle to poke a hole through its plastic base. Then thread a 6 in. (15 cm) piece of 0.6 mm wire through the hole and wrap it around the flower base a few times. Leave a wire tail to attach to the headband base.

3. Wind the wire tails tightly around the headband base to attach the flowers in the arrangement that looks best to you.

The Accent Flowers (steps 4–6)

4. Get the other, smaller flowers ready to attach to the headband base by pulling out their plastic centers and replacing them with crystal beads and sequins.

1.

2.

4.

5. You'll create the crystal bead and sequin center clusters using the same technique you used for the Jeweled Branches Necklace (page 63). Once you're done adding beads and sequins to the clusters, twist the two ends of the wire together and push the ends through the center of the flower so that they're ready to wrap around the headband base.

5a.

6. Once all the small flowers are ready, arrange them around the larger flowers and wrap the wires from the center clusters around the headband base to secure them.

7. When you're happy with your design, make sure all the wire ends are tightly wrapped around the headband base, tuck any loose ends in place with the pliers, and file down any sharp ends.

5b.

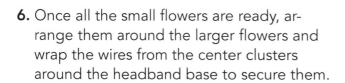

CREATIVE TIP

BA-DA-BLING!
Feeling more Lady Night than Lady Day? If you're making this headband for prom or some other extra fancy event, thread some more sparkly beads onto beading wire to make branches that you can wrap onto the headband so that they frame one side of your face.

SPARKLE-AND-CHAIN NECKLACE

YOU WILL NEED:

- ⟲ An antique brooch (with the pin backing removed: See Royal Jewels Necklace on page 30)
- ⟲ 6 ft (2 m) of 0.8 mm wire
- ⟲ A necklace chain or ribbon
- ⟲ 20–30 sparkly crystal beads, sequins, or semiprecious stones
- ⟲ Pliers
- ⟲ Two jump rings
- ⟲ A file
- ⟲ Superglue (optional)

When a sparkly brooch just isn't enough to advertise your fabulousness, the Sparkle-and-Chain Necklace takes bling to the next level. By adding some delicate tendrils of bejeweled wirework, you can create a necklace that'll make you look even more stunning. Wear it with a scoop- or V-necked dress, but most important, wear it with confidence.

CREATIVE TIP

DO YOUR 'DO
Got a fabulous 'do you want to highlight? You can easily transform this project into a beautiful hairpiece. Instead of creating loops to attach the chain to, just wrap the ends and cut off any excess wire. Then, you can either use superglue to attach a barrette underneath the brooch, or use bobby pins to secure the wirework to your hair. *Voilà*! Bling for your bouffant, braids, or bun.

1. Cut a 23 in. (60 cm) piece of wire and make a loop in one end by wrapping the wire back around itself a few times.

2. Thread your first bead onto the wire. Wrap the wire around the bead in a "C" shape to hold it in place about 1/2 in. (1 cm) from the loop.

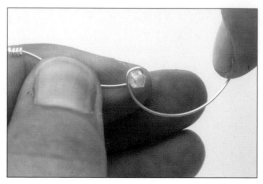

2.

3. Using your thumb and pointer finger, smooth the wire into a decorative curve and add your next bead. Hold the bead in place by wrapping the wire around the bead in a "C" shape. As you move on to the next bead, you might want to curve the wire in the opposite direction from the first curve so that the next bead is in a different position than the first.

4a.

4. After putting on three beads you're ready to add your brooch. If you want your brooch to be off center, add a few more beads before attaching it. You're aiming to make the whole piece 4–8 in. (10–20 cm) long. Before attaching your brooch, remember to remove the pin backing (see the Royal Jewels Necklace on page 30). Weave the wire through the open parts of the brooch until it's securely attached.

4b.

4c.

5. If you want a more elaborate design, go back in the other direction and keep adding beads, using the same technique as before. Every 1–1 1/2 in. (3–4 cm), wrap the wire around the first wire to hold it in place. You can also skip the step of making a wire "C" around the beads and hold them in place later with a drop of superglue. When you're done with the wirework, wrap the end of your wire around one of your loops a few times to secure it. Squeeze it with your pliers to make sure it's nice and tight.

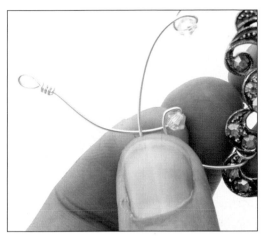

5a.

6. When you're happy with your design, cut a necklace chain in the middle and attach each end to your loops with jump rings. If you're using a ribbon, simply thread the ribbon through the loops and tie it around your neck.

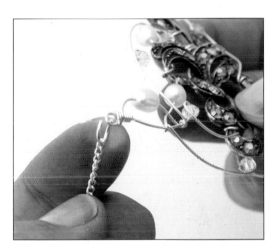

6.

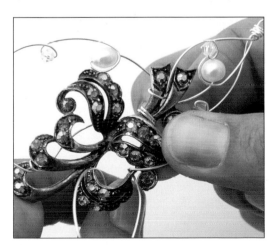

6a.

ART DECO BRACELET

YOU WILL NEED:

- ❂ 5–7 round or oval vintage beads (pearl or crystal beads work well)
- ❂ About 13 ft (4 m) of 0.6 mm wire
- ❂ 4–6 jump rings
- ❂ A lobster clasp
- ❂ Pliers
- ❂ A file

The Art Deco Bracelet is a project designed with the belief that wrists deserve to get dressed up just as much as necks do. Emerging in Paris in the twenties, the Art Deco style influenced everything from elegant and modern buildings to clothing and jewelry. With its beautiful geometric curves, this wire-wrapped bracelet looks super sophisticated and fancy without being over-the-top.

1. Cut a 20 in. (50 cm) piece of wire and bend it about 2 in. (5 cm) from one end. Make a loop in the bent end by wrapping the wire back around itself a few times. You should have a short wire tail left over from making the loop. Wrap the tail down the wire eight times and cut off the remaining tail end.

2. Thread a bead onto the long end of the wire so that it sits up against the wrapped wire section. With your eye, measure how far the bead is from the first loop and then make another loop at the other end of the wire, an equal distance from the bead. Wrap the wire tail from that loop around the wire eight times, but this time don't cut off the remaining long tail end.

3. Bend the long tail end of wire around the bottom of the bead and loop it around the top of the wrapped wire, so that the length of wire sticks out up the top of the bead and the side of the bead hugged by the wire is at the bottom.

4. Bend the wire snuggly over the top of the bead, just like you did on the bottom, and loop it around the top of the wrapped wire, so that the wire is ready to go around the bottom of the bead again.

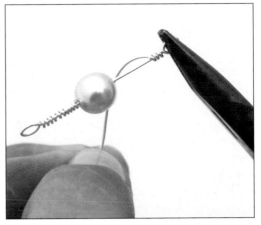

2.

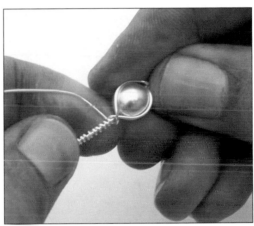

3.

5. Bend the wire under the bottom of the bead, pressing it behind the initial wire so that it doesn't stick out too much. Loop the wire around the wrapped wire section to the outside of the one you did before, then take the wire back over the top of the bead again.

6. Continue using this technique until you've covered all eight initial wire wrappings and the wire reaches the loops on both ends. Wrap the wire once more next to the loop and cut off the tail. Squeeze this last wrap with your pliers to secure it, and file down the sharp end.

7. Use this technique to make four or five more wrapped beads, depending on how long your want your bracelet to be.

8. Join the beads you've made by connecting the loops with jump rings. At one end of the bracelet, attach a lobster clasp to the loop with a jump ring. *Voilà!* An Art Deco masterpiece.

5.

CREATIVE TIP

DECO FOR YOUR NECK-O
You can use the same wire-wrapping technique to transform a really big and beautiful bead into a single Deco-inspired pendant. Just attach either end to the center of a necklace chain. Deco-tastic.

SPARKLING VINES HEADBAND

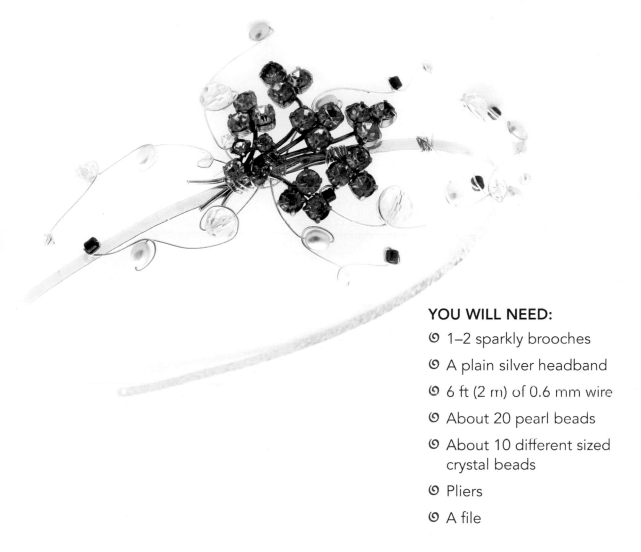

YOU WILL NEED:

- 1–2 sparkly brooches
- A plain silver headband
- 6 ft (2 m) of 0.6 mm wire
- About 20 pearl beads
- About 10 different sized crystal beads
- Pliers
- A file

It's like the Sparkle-and-Chain Necklace (page 83), but for your hair. The glamorous brooch and delicate vine-like wirework make this headband perfect for an up or down hairdo. A little randomness and asymmetry make the design even more of a feast for the eyes. Wear this sparkling beauty when you want everyone to understand what you already know: You're a queen.

1. Start your design about 4 in. (10 cm) from one end of the headband base so that the main part of the design will sit above your ear. Cut an 8 in. (20 cm) piece of wire and wrap the middle of the wire around the headband base four times.

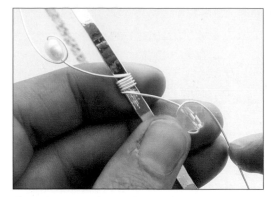

2.

2. Thread a pearl or crystal onto one of the wire ends and push it down to about a 1/2–1 in. (1–3 cm) away from the headband base. Wrap the wire around the bead in a "C" shape to keep it in place.

3. Using your thumb and pointer finger, smooth the wire into a decorative curve and thread on another bead. Wrap the wire around the bead in a "C" shape to secure it. You might want to curve the wire in the opposite direction as you did the first time so this bead is in a different position than the first one.

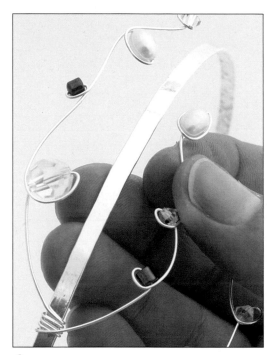

4.

4. Using this same technique, add two or three more beads to the wire. When you get to the end of your wire, secure the last bead by wrapping the wire around it, turning the "C" shape into an "O" shape, and wrapping the wire back around itself a few times to hold the bead in place.

5. Repeat steps two through four on the other wire end.

6. Create as many beaded wire vines as you want, varying the length of the wires. Bend the short ones around your face and let the longer ones go backward into your hair.

7. When you're satisfied with your beaded wire vines, you're ready to attach your brooch. You might need to remove the pin backing (see the Royal Jewels Necklace on page 30).

8. Cut a 6 in. (15 cm) piece of wire and thread it through a gap at one end of the brooch. Wrap the short end of the wire around the headband base a few times to secure it, then take the longer end to the other end of the brooch, thread it though a gap, and wrap the wire around the headband base to secure that end.

9. Cut off the tail end of the wire, squeeze it to the headband base with the pliers to secure it, and file down any sharp ends.

CREATIVE TIP

ANTIQUE LACE HEADBAND
If you've got big hair, or are looking for an even fancier look, add more wirework "vines" on the other side of the headband. And don't be afraid to bend the vines once the headband is in place. Part of the fun is arranging the design to suit your 'do.

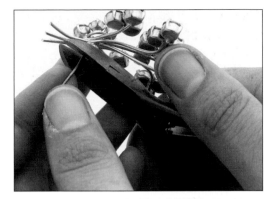

7.

8.

9.

ANTIQUE LACE HEADBAND

YOU WILL NEED:

- A medium-sized piece of lace
- White glue
- Manicure/nail scissors
- 6 in. (15 cm) of 0.6 mm and 3 ft (1 m) of 0.4 mm wire
- About 30 crystal and pearl beads
- 1–2 antique brooches
- A headband
- Pliers
- A file
- Water

When diamonds and pearls aren't enough, you need a little lace. This headband is the perfect combination of sweet and sassy: Delicate lace is balanced out with a little bling and an asymmetrical attitude. Wear it to make a casual dress a little fancier, or to add the finishing touch to your prom gown.

1. Dip your lace in a mixture of glue and water to stiffen it (see the Vintage Lace Choker on page 33). Once it's dry, use nail scissors to cut the glue out of the open parts of the design.

2. Cut a 12 in. (30 cm) piece of 0.4 mm wire and wrap one end around the headband base three times, about 2 in. (5 cm) from one end.

3. Using your thumb and pointer finger, smooth the wire into a decorative curve. Thread a pearl or crystal bead into the curve and wrap the wire around the bead in a "C" shape to keep it in place.

4. Thread the wire down through one end of the lace, wrap it once around the headband base, and thread the wire through to the front of the lace to attach another bead.

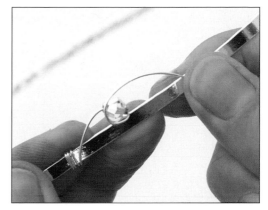

3.

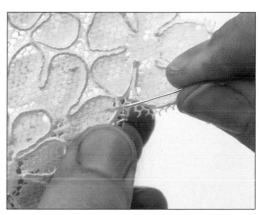

4.

CREATIVE TIP

FEATHERS IN YOUR CAP
If you feel like your headband is lacking a certain *je ne sais quoi*, consider attaching some wire "vines" to the headband (see the Sparkling Vines Headband on page 89). Or, for a funkier look, try tucking some small feathers underneath the brooch (you can secure them to the lace with a little drop of super glue at the base of the feathers).

5. Thread on another bead, secure it with the wire "C," and poke the wire back down through the lace, this time wrapping it around the headband base toward the middle of the lace. Continue adding beads and wrapping around the headband base until you reach the other end of the lace. Secure the wire a final time by wrapping it around the headband base three times.

6. Attach a new piece of 0.4 mm wire to the headband base and weave it through the lace, curving the wire and attaching beads along the way using the same technique as before. Add as much or as little beaded wire as you want, depending on how elaborate you want your design to be. Be sure to leave a blank space for your brooch. When you're done adding the beaded wire, secure the wire by wrapping it around the headband base three times.

7. Before attaching your brooch, remember to remove the pin backing (see the Royal Jewels Necklace on page 30). Loop a 6 in. (15 cm) piece of 0.6 mm wire through a gap in one end of the brooch and wrap the wire around the headband base a few times to secure it, then do the same at the other end of the brooch. Feel along your headband base for poking wires and file down any sharp ends. Now you have a lovely lacy hair accessory.

5.

7.

GOLDEN TOUCH TIARA

YOU WILL NEED:

- A colorful vintage brooch
- Three small branches of fake leaves spray-painted gold
- A plain gold tiara base (Tip: If you can't find a tiara base, you can bend a headband into a more circular shape.)
- 6 ft (2 m) of 0.6 mm gold wire
- Pearls, crystals, and other beads to match your brooch
- Superglue
- Pliers
- A file

Warning: Do not attempt this project unless your inner diva is ready to break free. The Golden Touch Tiara is pure magic: a mix of vintage brooches, leaves, beads, and fancy wirework. Once you rest this baby on your head, everything you touch is bound to turn to gold. You might be inclined to think this kind of tiara is only for very special occasions, but we dare you to wear it the next time you run an errand. Sure, people might be staring at you, but that's only because they can't believe a celebrity is wandering around the frozen food aisle.

1. Start by adding the tallest parts to the tiara. About 4 in. (10 cm) from one end of the tiara base, wrap the midpoint of a 6 in. (15 cm) piece of wire around the base four times. Trim the right end of the wire so that it is 1 in. (3 cm) shorter than the left end.

2. Cut a 4 in. (10 cm) piece of wire and wrap the midpoint of it around the tiara base 1 in. (3 cm) to the left of where you wrapped the first wire.

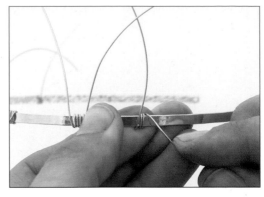

2.

3. Use your thumb and pointer finger to curve one of these wires in the same direction as the longest wire, as if it were growing toward the center of the tiara. Loop the other piece of wire around the tiara base and gently bend it as if it were growing upward.

4. Add another 4 in. (10 cm) wire in this same way 1 in. (3 cm) to the right of where you wrapped the first wire. Repeat step three with this wire.

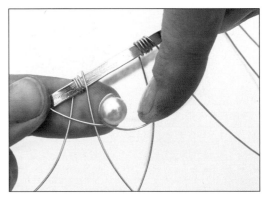

6.

5. Depending on how elaborate you want your design, add more wires farther to the left along the tiara base. Make them shorter than the first wires, but not too short, as you'll be bending small loops on the ends of the wires later on.

6. Cut a 20 in. (50 cm) piece of wire and wrap one end of it around the right side of the tiara base a few times, about 2 in. (5 cm) from the end. Thread a bead onto the long end of the wire and wrap the wire around it in a "C" shape to keep it in place. Using your thumb and pointer finger, smooth the wire into a decorative curve before threading on the next bead.

7. Continue using this curving and beading technique along the tiara base, wrapping the wire around the tiara base every 1 in. (3 cm) to keep it secure. Once you get to the other side of the tiara base, stop about 2 in. (5 cm) from the end. Wrap the wire around the base a few times before heading back in the direction you came from. Use the same curving and beading technique, but this time make the curves higher and add more beads. Go back and forth across the tiara base until your design is as elaborate as you want it to be.

8.

8. When you get back to where you started, wrap the wire around the tiara base a few times, cut off the tail end of the wire, and squeeze the wire to the tiara base with the pliers to secure it.

9a.

9. Now you're ready to attach your brooch to the tiara. Remember to remove the pin backing (see the Royal Jewels Necklace on page 30). Thread a 4 in. (10 cm) piece of wire through the back of the brooch, then wrap both ends of the wire tightly around the tiara base to secure it. Cut off the tail ends.

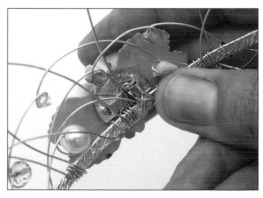

9b.

10. Choose small beads to attach to the tops of the wires. If your beads are too large they might get the look of a bug's antennae. Thread one bead onto each high wire and make a small loop at the top of the wire to keep the bead from falling off. Hold the tiara so that the beads slide up next to the tiara base, put a small drop of superglue next to each loop, and quickly push the beads onto the glue.

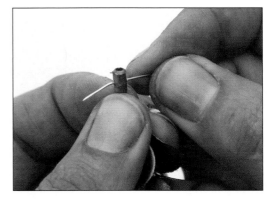

10.

11. Now add the gold-sprayed leaves. Wrap a 4 in. (10 cm) piece of wire a few times around each leaf base, and then wrap the wire around the tiara base. Cut off the tail ends and squeeze the wires tightly to the tiara base with the pliers to secure them. Eat your heart out, King Midas!

11a.

11b.

USEFUL WEBSITES

SUPPLIES

www.beadaholique.com

www.jewelrysupply.com

www.arizonabeadcompany.com

www.beadingusa.com

www.beadwholesaler.com

www.fusionbeads.com

www.artbeads.com

www.firemountaingems.com

www.diy-hair-combs.com (headband and tiara bases)

www.agrainofsand.com (vintage beads)

www.beadessence.com (vintage beads)

www.dollsandlace.com (vintage lace)

www.shrinkydinks.com (Shrinky Dinks)

SELLING YOUR WORK

www.beadage.net/selling (tips for selling jewelry online)

www.ebay.com

www.etsy.com

INDEX

ABOUT THE AUTHOR

Sarah Drew teaches at the Mid Cornwall School of Jewellery and at St. Austell College. She specializes in wirework and her recycled jewelry and vintage headress workshops are very popular. She sells her jewelry through galleries, fashion boutiques, and bridal shops across the United Kingdom, as well as directly from her website, www.sarahdrew.com. She has supplied jewelry to stores such as Liberty, Harrods, and Brown Bride in London, and her work is frequently featured in magazines.

MORE FROM ZEST BOOKS

SCHOOL LIFE

97 Things to Do Before You Finish High School
by Steven Jenkins & Erika Stalder

Been There, Survived That
Getting Through Freshman Year of High School
edited by Karen Macklin

Crap
How to Deal With Annoying Teachers, Bosses, Backstabbers,
and Other Stuff that Stinks
by Erin Elisabeth Conley, Karen Macklin, & Jake Miller

The Dictionary of High School B.S.
From Acne to Varsity, All the Funny, Lame,
and Annoying Aspects of High School Life
by Lois Beckwith

Freshman
Tales of 9th Grade Obsessions, Revelations, and Other Nonsense
by Corinne Mucha

Take Me With You
Off-to-College Advice from One Chick to Another
by Nikki Roddy

Uncool
A Girl's Guide to MisFitting In
by Erin Elisabeth Conley

POP CULTURE

Dead Strange
The Truth Behind 50 Myths That Just Won't Die
by Matt Lamy

The End
50 Apocalyptic Visions From Pop Culture
That You Should Know About...before it's too late
by Laura Barcella

How to Fight, Lie, and Cry Your Way to Popularity (and a prom date)
Lousy Life Lessons from 50 Teen Movies
by Nikki Roddy

Reel Culture
50 Classic Movies You Should Know About
(So You Can Impress Your Friends)
by Mimi O'Connor

Scandalous!
50 Shocking Events You Should Know About
(So You Can Impress Your Friends)
by Hallie Fryd

DATING + RELATIONSHIPS

Crush
A Girl's Guide to Being Crazy in Love
by Erin Elisabeth Conley

The Date Book
A Girl's Guide to Going Out With Someone New
by Erika Stalder

Dumped
A Girl's Guide to Happiness After Heartbreak
by Erin Elisabeth Conley

Girls Against Girls
Why We Are Mean to Each Other, and How We Can Change
by Bonnie Burton

Kiss
A Girl's Guide to Puckering Up
by Erin Elisabeth Conley

The Mother Daughter Cookbook
Recipes to Nourish Relationships
by Lynette Rohrer Shirk

Queer
The Ultimate LGBT Guide for Teens
by Kathy Belge & Marke Bieschke

Split In Two
Keeping It Together When Your Parents Live Apart
by Karen Buscemi

HEALTH 101

Girl in a Funk
Quick Stress Busters (and Why They Work)
by Tanya Napier & Jenn Kollmer

Sex: A Book for Teens
An Uncensored Guide to Your Body, Sex, and Safety
by Nikol Hasler

Skin
The Bare Facts
by Lori Bergamotto

STYLE

The Book of Styling
An Insider's Guide to Creating Your Own Look
by Somer Flaherty

Fashion 101
A Crash Course in Clothing
by Erika Stalder

The Look Book
50 Iconic Beauties and How to Achieve Their Signature Styles
by Erika Stalder

HOW-TO

47 Things You Can Do for the Environment
by Lexi Petronis

87 Ways to Throw a Killer Party
by Melissa Daly

Don't Sit on the Baby
The Ultimate Guide to Sane, Skilled, and Safe Babysitting
by Halley Bondy

Girl in a Fix
Quick Beauty Solutions (and Why They Work)
by Somer Flaherty & Jenn Kollmer

Holy Spokes
A Biking Bible for Everyone
by Rob Coppilillo

Indie Girl
From Starting a Band to Launching a Fashion Company,
Nine Ways to Turn Your Creative Talent into Reality
by Arne Johnson & Karen Macklin

In the Driver's Seat
A Girl's Guide to Her First Car
by Erika Stalder

Jeaneology
Crafty Ways to Reinvent Your Old Blues
by Nancy Flynn

Junk-Box Jewelry
25 DIY Low Cost (or No Cost) Jewelry Projects
by Sarah Drew

Start It Up
The Complete Teen Business Guide to Turning Your Passions Into Pay
by Kenrya Rankin

Where's My Stuff
The Ultimate Teen Organizing Guide
by Samantha Moss with Lesley Schwartz

TRUE STORIES

Dear Teen Me
Authors Write Letters to Their Teen Selves
edited by Miranda Kenneally & E. Kristin Anderson

Regine's Book
A Teen Girl's Last Words
by Regine Stokke

Zoo Station
The Story of Christiane F.
by Christiane F.